WonderWorks

Decodable Reader

Unit 6

McGraw Hill

Contents

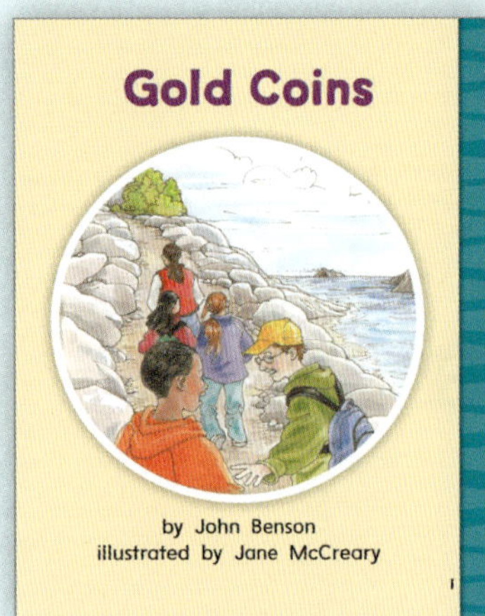
Gold Coins
by John Benson
illustrated by Jane McCreary
1

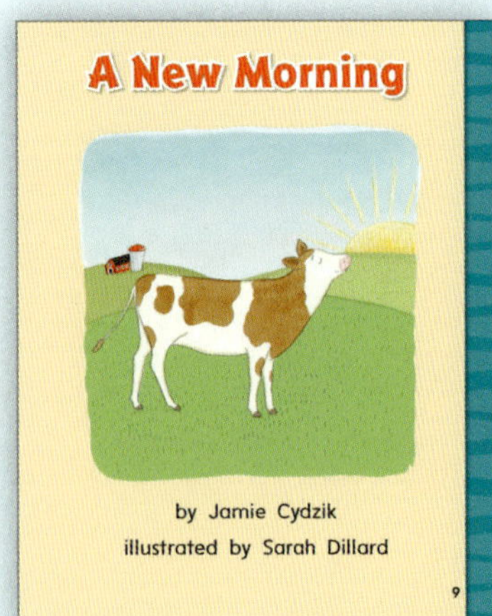
A New Morning
by Jamie Cydzik
illustrated by Sarah Dillard
9

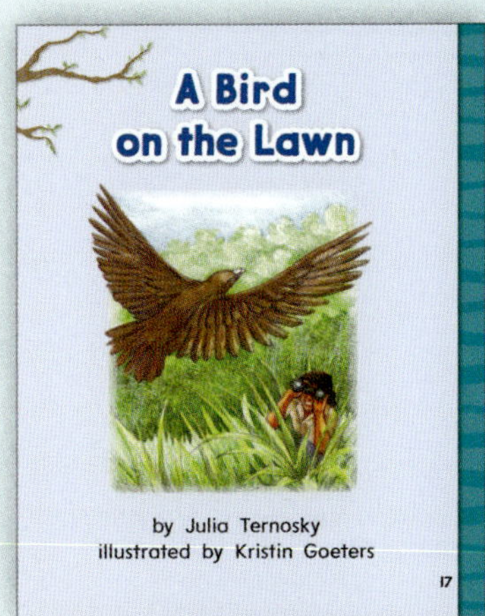
A Bird on the Lawn
by Julia Ternosky
illustrated by Kristin Goeters
17

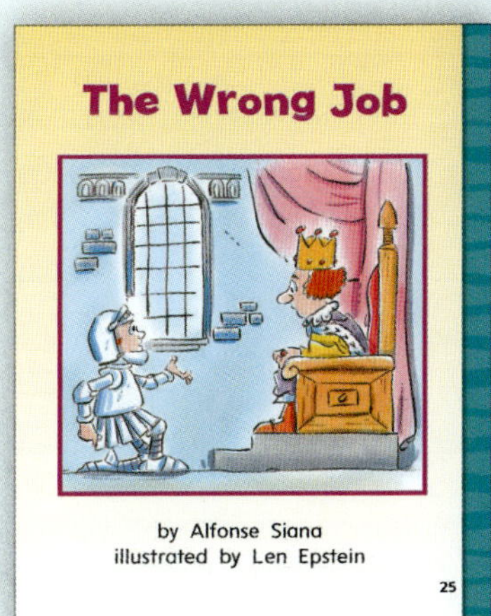
The Wrong Job
by Alfonse Siana
illustrated by Len Epstein
25

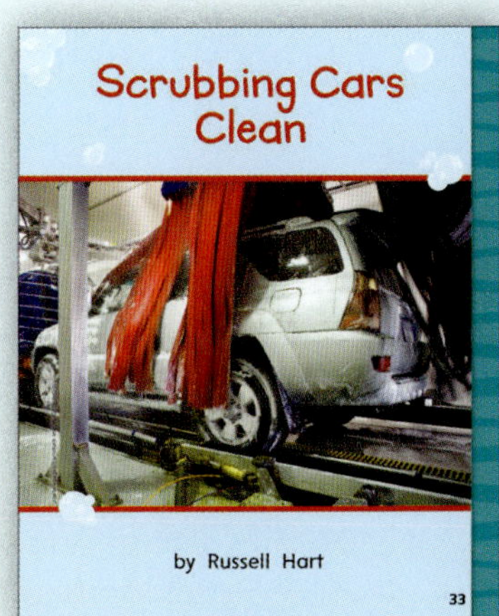
Scrubbing Cars Clean
by Russell Hart
33

Gold Coins

by John Benson
illustrated by Jane McCreary

We looked out. The rain had stopped. It had not spoiled the hike.

"Let's go!" Joyce called in a happy voice.

We looked at the water.

Lucy pointed. "Look up **above**! It's a rainbow."

We gazed at the rainbow.

We hiked to a lighthouse.
We tried not to slip and **fall**.

Joyce told us lighthouses help ships avoid rocks. That's why we **build** them on the coast.

Waves crashed on the rocks and made a loud noise.

Joyce joined Floyd. She said, "Those rocks sunk a ship. It was filled with gold coins."

Floyd thought, "Maybe I will find gold coins."

He looked at the sandy soil. He walked **toward** a shiny, bright thing. Was it **money**?

Floyd looked closer. Then he **knew** that it was just an old candy paper made of foil.

"I'll keep looking," said Floyd. He smiled. Joyce smiled back.

A New Morning

by Jamie Cydzik

illustrated by Sarah Dillard

Ruth the cow likes morning time. She can feel fresh dew on the grass. She squints her **eyes**. The Sun is bright in the blue sky.

Each morning, she checks on all the animals.

The farm is a **busy** place.
Ruth sees Bruce the sheep.
He is fixing his wooly poof.
"Moo!" says Ruth. "Good
morning!"

Ruth is in a good mood!
She **brought** Luke the pig
fruit to chew.
"Yum!" says Ruth. "Enjoy
your food!"

Ruth spots June the pup.
Oh no, June looks hot!
Ruth can help. "Is there
enough water? Stay cool!"
says Ruth.

Sue the hen opens her coop **door**. She scoops up her new chicks. Ruth waves to them.

"Hello!" **answer** the chicks.

Ruth rests by a few pretty blooms. She sees loons in the pond. She has checked on all of her friends.

"Moo!" says Ruth. "The day will start soon!"

A Bird on the Lawn

by Julia Ternosky
illustrated by Kristin Goeters

I **love** birds. My **brother** gave me a book about them.

In the book, I saw a **picture** of a bunting. It's a small bird with a short tail and beak.

I got up at five this morning.

My **father** taught me that birds wake up at dawn.

I walked in the woods. I crawled in itchy tall grass. Awful bugs flew around me.

I saw many things, but I did not spot a bunting.

Small birds squawked and cawed. They flew away fast. Was it because of me?

No. I spotted a hawk. It was looking for food.

I drove home. I felt sad. I did not see a bunting.

When I got home, I came to a halt in my driveway. A bunting was on my lawn!

I got out of my car and paused. I saw another bunting on my awning. Is this the **mother**? Maybe it is a **friend**.

I saw two buntings today!

The Wrong Job

by Alfonse Siana
illustrated by Len Epstein

Each **month**, King Knox asked his knight to perform a task.

He said, "Can you tie knots?"

"No," said Knight Waldo.

King Knox asked, "Can you sharpen this knife?"

Knight Waldo replied, "No, but I can butter homemade bread for all of the **children**."

"Can you knit socks for me?" asked King Knox.

"I do not know how, but I can pile this wool into a soft bed," said Knight Waldo.

A **year** passed. King Knox gnashed his teeth. Then he knocked on the knight's door.

He shouted, "Let me ask a **question**. What can you do?"

The knight kneeled down on one knee. He said, "This is the wrong job for me."

King Knox and Waldo knew **their** time together was done.

Waldo wrote a note to King Knox. He quit his job. Then he packed a knapsack and left. He started a sheep farm. "I should have **been** doing this all along," sang Waldo.

Scrubbing Cars Clean

Jupiterimages/Comstock Images/Getty Images

by Russell Hart

Jupiterimages/Comstock Images/Getty Images